Khorde Rushen

Keith Dowman

Dzogchen Now! Books
2020

A Dzogchen Now! Book
www.keith.dowman@gmail.com

© Keith Dowman 2020

ISBN:9798646399626

Font set in Book Antiqua 10.5

Contents

Introduction

The Dzogchen Mandala is already established. It is the ground of our being, pre-existing our birth, underlying our lives, and welcoming our demise. Everything that we know physically, energetically and mentally arises out of that Dzogchen mandala and retreats into it. In the confusion of our lives that mandala, an expanse without center or boun-dary, has become lost to sight. The khordé rushen practice is designed to bring it back into ground-awareness. This extremely potent yoga is unique to Dzogchen.

First, we are caught up on the wheel of life with samsara and nirvana inextricably confused, with a dualistically formulated intellect that is painful. Sakya-muni described it as the suffering that attends human life. The khordé rushen is a Dzogchen yoga overcoming that suffering. The literal translation of khordé rushen – 'establishing the unity of the samsara and nirvana dualism' – states the problem and the answer. We may know already that any separation is impossible, that the unity of samsara and nirvana is realized in initiatory experience, that the enlightened mind of *rigpa* implies a unitary state of being. To know this in our bones, to realize it existentially, is the purpose of the khorde rushen. But to begin the practice that is to give us absolute certainty in the unitary great perfection of Dzogchen we assume the separation of samsara and nirvana that the dualizing intellect insists upon. Assuming that the natural state of being has been undone, we seek to clarify the duality of samsara and nirvana by acting it out.

We begin with the certainty that mind and the nature of mind are identical, that *rigpa* defines reality as experiential-unitary subjective and objective aspects. That enlightened realization can be stated as 'samsara is nirvana', that

nondual experience is knowledge of buddha and knowledge of the nature of mind. We know that samsara and
nirvana refer to the two sides of a single coin, that in
reality we cannot have one without the other – or to say it
without equivocation, quite distinctly – they are identical.
That certainty arises with the intuition of the ground of
being.

We know it, but it is not proven in our moment to moment
experience. A strong karmic current reinforcing our habit of
dualistic perception infuses our every experience. For that
reason, we attempt to make a distinction between samsara
and nirvana, to separate samsara and nirvana. In order to
know that the duality is a unity, we need to know the
duality intimately. The initial, primary part of the rushen
is to focus the samsaric forms and in that effort proving
that they cannot be separated from nirvana. The second
part, identified with nirvana, is to prove that nirvana
cannot be separated from a samsaric form. The result is to
strengthen the certainty of the transcendent awareness in
which samsara and nirvana are one.

In the first and principal part of the rushen, circumstance,
intention and inspiration providing heightened awareness, like stretching a slack elastic band to its limit, or
cultivating a fallow field we illuminate the potential of the
wheel of life, which is a metaphoric way of saying we
playback our psychic potential, repressed memories and
fantasies, hopes and fears in the strong natural light of
day. We bring out of the darkness into the light the
'unopened' subconscious impressions laid down from
birth until the present time (or the end of time). In this
process of enlightenment we eliminate major sources of
karmic causation. Through simultaneous loosening,
illuminating and abandoning intractable concepts and
fixed notions we eradicate karmic propensity.

Secondly, in that process, opening hitherto closed areas of memory, illuminating what has hitherto been seen as through a glass darkly, we expand experience of ourselves in an enlightened world. Further, identifying with the root of mind – aka the ground of being – we set ourselves up to allow vastly more experience to filter through into consciousness than previously. Or, to say it another way, our heavens are higher and our hells deeper and we delve ever wider into the vast potential that the wheel of life affords.

Thirdly, through the dramatic quality of the rushen exercise, by being in it but not of it, we are elevated into a transcendent sphere where we can relax fully in its aftermath, which is called the *'neduwa'* (see 'Crucial endgame' p.24). The amateur actor is in danger of identifying so heartily with his theatrical persona that he loses all sense of reality and becoming his rôle he takes on its karma. On the other hand, being in it but not of it he opens himself to identity with a controlling ego. The egolessness of initiatory experience frees the yogi from both these dangers.

In the second and final part of the practice, enacting nirvana, or rather, gaining a taste of nirvana in the state of complete exhaustion (*neduwa*) in the aftermath of intense practice of acting out samsara, we have reached a place of nonaction, literal non-activity, wherein the body is exhausted, the energetic body is at rest, and the mind, sense of self shattered, allows its intrinsic nature to filter through.

Thus, attempting to separate what is inseparable, we come to the realization that what we have here and now is as perfect as it can be. Existentially, however, if extraction of the essence and separation of samsara from nirvana is what the khorde rushen achieves, the product is the natural condition of being, the great perfection, Dzogchen itself.

***

Some commentators have distinguished between an outer and an inner rushen. This khorde rushen is what is known also as the outer rushen and it is practiced literally both physically and vocally in the great outside, implying interaction with the natural environment, with the elements, the weather, and flora and fauna. In that sense this rushen is 'outer', as opposed to the inner rushen that is practiced sitting on a cushion in front of an altar. Perhaps the latter method represents a more subtle approach, more attuned to the monk in his cell who has his food and water served him twice a day. This khorde rushen, meanwhile, is more appropriate for the yogi/yogini who has taken human karma with all its crass tendencies and foibles as the vehicle in which to ride from birth to death sitting on the magic carpet of the perfected moment.

However, it may be that we are attuned to the music of the lower realms, that the music of higher spheres has lost its charm. Or perhaps the dualistic vision preferred by our social and political guardians to protect us from the wide world of karmic potential has proved only too painful in its actuality, failing in its promise, and occasional glimpses and taste of the underlying basis of the wheel of life has given us more joy. Whatever our karmic history, the khorde rushen provides a view and a practice that in its welcome inclusivity is liberating. In its attempted separation of objective and subjective aspects of unitary awareness it gives us full-bodied satisfaction.

To say it another way, in the khorde rushen we are urged to acknowledge both genetic and conditioned aspects of our present life-experience, and in its manifestation we are moved to celebrate it. Whatever caste or class habits, whatever educational and religious predilections (or lack thereof), whatever moral and ethical stance (or absence thereof), whatever cultural proclivities, whatever social manners, have been acquired in our short lives, all is accepted and transcended, all is recognized as a veridical and true manifestation of mind's nature. As such, it not only brings us joy but the strength of realization and awareness.

Transcending our conditioning, accepting karma for whatever it is, we are free of it. That freedom implies immediate release of the pressures of karmic tendency, although repeated and profound airing of it is required for total annihilation of it. The overriding value of awareness is 'recog-nition'. To recognize the forms of our conditioned being and know the mind behind the many masks; to break through the traps formed by habitual thought structures and emotional reaction and to breathe life and with it potential for change into subconscious karmic patterns, to realize the impossibility of grasping and controlling the underlying dynamic of being and knowing such realization as bliss, that is the awareness-potential in the khorde rushen. Simple awareness of a putative infrastructure (that can never be substantiated), with an infinite potency (that can never be validated), provides confidence in the now to rest freely (*chogzhak*). Here we are released from the karmic tendencies instigated and reinforced by past action to reach out, to grasp and hold what we like and what we want.

Practicing the khorde rushen, experience as memory, hopes and fears, will arise in the raw. The tradition provides labels and images to identify them, all nicely arranged in what is called the 'wheel of life'. At the wheel's hub, cock, snake and pig represent positive, negative or neutral response to all sensory impressions; outside that hub the wheel's six spokes apportion enough space for figurative repres-entation of the karmic outcome of the six basic emotional responses – desire, anger, fear, jealousy, pride and attach-ment. The outer concentric band of the wheel is divided into twelve parts representing the twelve interdependent elements of conditioned existence. The entire wheel of samsaric possibility is held by the Great Black ungovernable force of karmic inevitability (Mahakala). This wheel is a mnemonic device providing the means of identifying and labelling the elements of our experience as they enter consciousness in our khorde rushen praxis.

On the wheel of life, the aspects of emotional response – attachment, rejection, negativity, inflation, deflation, and affectivity – are represented figuratively by caricatured beings inhabiting our psychic dimension, namely, 'hungry ghosts', 'hell-beings' 'animals', 'gods', 'demonic anti-gods', and 'human beings'. Each form of being is designated by color: divine beings are yellow, titanic anti-gods are green, human beings are orange, animals are grey, 'hungry ghosts' are red; hell-beings are blue: all colors are opaque and dense. These archetypal caricatures are useful to characterize and label subjective experience as it emerges into consciousness; their use is expanded when they become the prop of memory-infiltrated ideas inducing imagination that is then acted out in dance and sound in the khorde rushen theatre.

In this way, the outer rushen retreat is a primary technique for the clarification of mind. By attempting to separate samsara from nirvana, with its implication of release from the former into the latter, we have re-established with finality the identity of samsara as nirvana and nirvana as samsara. This is accomplished both through time and in the timeless moment, and may be restated as intuitively identifying ordinary mind with *rigpa*. Metaphorically this may be iterated as the recognition of *rigpa* as the mirror while awareness is the glass and mind is the image in the glass.

While those images state the ultimate purpose and product of khorde rushen, relative benefits also emerge, such as experience of body, speech and mind as empty form and thus the reduction in attachment to that form. Inevitably, our scope of experience expands to include increasingly greater knowledge of the actual and potential forms of our conditioned being. In that constantly enlarging experience, predispositions, proclivities and habit patterns are brought into detached awareness and with success in the practice eventually deracinated as clear light. In that process we are released from thought and emotional traps, and the inhibitions and blockages, and 'ghosts' caught in the subconscious are blown away. Hopes and fears dissolve, opening up the interior all-encompassing sphere of compassion, and thereby we realize that ignorance is the bliss of the nature of mind.

If these relative advantages appear to be aspects of the transcendence of conditioning, we can enlarge upon them by cataloguing moments of temporal experience that have been trapped in the subconscious effecting a shrinking and attenuation of direct experience, now to be purged in the catharsis of the rushen process. Firstly, the pre-birth and childhood experience leading to adolescent trauma may be recalled and released. Then the social values instilled by formal education, ethical values by church perhaps, or the moral and family values imparted at home are reviewed, filtered and possibly rejected entirely. Likewise, the manner of sitting, eating and drinking, the way of loving and copulating, and the style of conversing, all modulated by the peer group, are reconsidered. This partial list documents only a fraction of the contents of the all-inclusive Dzogchen mandala. Each of us has his/her own extraordinary, unique karma to be excavated out of the vastness of that mandala and it is precisely that vastness which is potentially exposed and made aware in the khorde rushen.

If the nature of mind is approached through articulated sound and form in this primary part of the practice, then in the second part, the neduwa, in which in nirvana unconsciously we are identified with the nature of mind through 'nonaction', sound and form arise spontaneously as the moment requires, and yet again *maya* and the nature of mind are one and the same.

During the formal practice, at the conclusion of each section defined by one of the six realms, we recall the bodhisattva vow by taking on the sins of the beings in that realm. Insofar as we began the practice with the refuge and celebration of the enlightened mind with the bodhisattva vow implicit if not vocalized, that vow has been with us throughout the practice. The khorde rushen is performed for both self and others and it is just as well to remind ourselves of it occasionally during the practice.

                              ***

Part One provides the manner of practice of the three options for khorde rushen. It constitutes personal advice required for a prolonged retreat. Part Two comprises material from two great masters and exponents of the tradition, Jigme Lingpa and Jamgon Kongtrul, with crystal clear instructions on the principles of practice in the Tibetan tradition. I have included transcripts of my talks – pep-talks – given to practitioners about to begin rushen retreats. The final item was written for yogins whose primary concern in the retreat was sexual and who required inspiration for practice.

The conditions for practice in the West are quite different from those that existed for Tibetans in their own land before the Chinese occupation. The temporal and spatial para-meters of the outer rushen practice in old Tibet are unavailable to us in the West and need to be rethought. The tradition may be reconstituted, but the basic principles will remain unchanged. The two transcripts I have included in Part Two are of talks given to practitioners camped in a forested area at least one hundred meters apart, (optionally) meeting in silence twice daily for food. This evidently is a compromise on the Himlalayan version of the practice. Creative imagination and resolution are required to give the practice the environment that it deserves.

Where did the khorde rushen originate? The term 'rushen' has no known Indic equivalent, so we must assume an indigenous Tibetan origin, probably Bon. Certainly, we know of no such practice existing in sanskritic India. It seems, however, eminently suited to the West in the 21st century. At the time of the corona virus pandemic, it should be noted, the 'classical' solitary practice is the appropriate form of the rushen, if only a solitary place outside social constraints can be found.

Part One: The Practice

Initial Considerations

Place: primarily, the place of practice must be in solitude, without proximity to habitation, and without roads or paths passing by. Ideally, it should have a water source close by and shade from the sun is essential. A visual panorama providing a sense of space is desirable. This ideal place is far distant, it may be in the jungle, or in the mountains or desert where there is space, or at least spaciousness.

Season: the climate should be temperate, neither too hot nor too cold, free from rain and snow, neither in wet monsoon nor in high summer heat.

Solitude: the crucial factor is solitude, far from the madding crowd. Abandon electronic devices of all kinds. Communication with the outside world is to be strictly controlled.

Secrecy: It is preferable not to advertise your activity. Once the rushen retreat has begun the fewer people aware of it the better.

Partners: retreating with a partner of the opposite sex makes the gender interaction primary, whether it is positive or negative, inclusive or rejective. This option should be very well considered and discussed with a guide.

Time: Through day and night, sessions should be of indeterminate length according to capacity and breaks also according to requirement.

Rules: solitude is essential, secrecy is primary; otherwise the crucial rule is to abandon all rules. Fasting is desirable.

Attitude: fearless, uninhibited, shameless, keeping the goal in mind: maintain nondiscrimination throughout. A sense of great opportunity should be maintained.

Psychedelics and Medicina: Initiatory experience have made chemical and herbal inducements irrelevant. The maxim is the less reliance on external elements the better. Dzogchen khorde rushen practice opens an inexhaustible primal internal energy source. If the yogin/yogini has presentiment of serious psychic blockages or finds it impossible to manage them with simple rushen, as a last resort he/she can fall back on a psychedelic rushen.

The Compromise: If you cannot practice alone for one reason or another, your second-best option is to join a group practice. In the West, this inadequate substitute has become standard.

The Seat: travelling or sedentary, alone or in a group, the seat is of primary importance. Both placement and comfort should be considered. Basic principles of *feng shui* may be useful; the Mexican shaman Don Juan discussed the crucial importance of the seat. Common sense goes a long way. A seat outside the dwelling is primary. A fallback seat under cover is desirable if the weather proves inclement.

Gathering Necessities: Regarding food and water, fasting heightens sensibility and awareness. Food should be basic and minimal. Unlimited clean water is essential. All necessary supplies should be carried in, or food should be otherwise arranged so that food and water does not become a distraction.

Protection: A ring of protection may be drawn around the area in which practice will take place. The protective circle keeps all negative influences out and keeps all positive influences in. With the circle of protection in place we can concentrate fully on internal concern which is the practice at hand.

Preliminary Ritual

The first session of the retreat, and optionally every day thereafter, should begin with extended preparatory practice. First, the area can be purified by offering of thrown rice (or other grain) to the 'spirits' and 'guardians' with cries of 'Lhagyelo! Lhagyelo!' and 'Khakha khahi!' 'Honor to the gods!' and 'Come! Eat! Be Content'! Offering to the buddha-mandala can be made with light, sound and symbolic substances.

Taking your prepared seat, make the nine breaths and take refuge in the nature of mind and celebrate buddha-enlightenment. Rehearse the bodhisattva vow and recall the four boundless states. Recall the four mind changes – precious human body, impermanence, karmic cause and effect and karmic inevitability (*lodro namparzhi*). Optionally, do the inner rushen clarification practices and purification of body, speech and mind.

Practice Options

The actual practice is to act out one's karma in solitude. This can be done in two ways with a possible third. The first, the Formal Practice, made with discipline, ritualistically, within a strict framework, is the classical, traditional manner (see the Tibetan texts pp.32-43). The second is that same practice liberated and performed, unstructured, artlessly and impulsively, also within a tight frame, which can be called unpremeditated or unstructured rushen. The third option is to take the practice into the home and social context, a practice effective only for practitioners living in a loose society outside the straight social norm. These three options may be performed separately, sequentially, or the one may blend into the next, particularly, the first into the second.

Formal Practice

Keep the sense of great opportunity in the forefront of the mind; keep the practice hidden, refrain from any exhibitionism. Maintain a fearless, uninhibited, shameless, attitude of nondiscrimination. Impose no limiting parameters – moral or aesthetic – on physical, vocal or mental activity. Maintain full awareness of whatever appears in the mind-sky and take on the pain of beings in the various realms that they may be released.

With the mind, imagine and visualize successively oneself living in each of the six realms upon the wheel of time. To begin, evoke each realm successively, employing memory of emotion and karma, and when that fails employ imagination.

With the voice, vocalize the six realms one after the other. Imagine the sounds of each realm; rehearse the pain of each of the lower realms: the screams of frustration, agony and fear. Vocalize the pleasures of the upper realms, purrs of sensory delight, shouts of victory, of release.

With the body, imagine and perform the various mudras (gestures) – unmoving postures – of the beings of the six realms. Sit in meditation, imitate the thinker, take on the mudras of divinity, and jealousy, pain, fear and subservience; invent the dances of the six realms; act out the dramas of each specific realm. Nudity, with or without dance, can introduce a valuable extra dimension to the rushen.

Use the expletive syllable PHAT to break the inevitable attachment, compulsion or obsession, or to free oneself from inability to move or speak. In case of fear and confusion, take refuge in Samantabhadra, the unity of all gurus.

The vignettes of the six realms below are intended to provide a starting point, and perhaps some inspiration, for the actual practice of acting out in succession the dynamics of their physical, energetic and mental aspects. Each practitioner knows the realms in a different way. In order for the rushen to be affective, each yogin/yogini must find the personal sources of the emotional syndromes that impede full awareness of those samsaric manifestations and turn them into nirvanic experience. To restate the process: what begins as a formal notion of the emotional root of a specific experiential syndrome, by connection with the memory of a lived experience, becomes a 'real' event. Viewed with the detachment that the meditation-situation lends the experience, the emotion is acted out as if by a competent professional actor, fully engaged with a situation but still not totally giving himself up to the game. 'In it but not of it' is the biblical phrase that describes it.

No fixed period for practice in each of the realms is given. Some sessions will pass quickly and easily, some will require lengthy involvement, while others will not even get off the ground. To apportion a couple of hours for a full session in which time the wheel may turn once, twice or thrice, is perhaps an average allotment.

Each of the following sections, each relating to one of the six realms, contains starting points for acting out part of the six-realm psychology. Each section provides suggestions – or keys – that can initiate a session of rushen: primarily, an emotion, then an allusion to a color, psychological state, and to sources of evocative imagery. Each section contains a list of suggestions of identification, metaphorical, allegorical or psychological, composed in the first-person pronoun, which can provide a take-off point for first-hand exploration of that particular realm. The realms need not be taken in the order provided.

In the Hell Realm

To enter, use thoughts of anger and hatred, memories of vile impotent rage, humiliation in shame and disgrace, in all extremely painful situations. Recognize the deep or dirty blue color. Recognize the natural potential for alienation and aversion in dualistic perception. Imagine wandering in depths of great pain amongst the beings of hell (use Dante's *Inferno* and Bosch's paintings.)

I am an alienated devil, aggressively and maliciously
       inflicting pain on others.
I am the victim of karma, suffering divine retribution.
I am lonely and lost, angry, lashing out in arbitrary
       violence.
Imagine: hot hells, cold hells, mountains of knives, grass
       and trees of swords, etc., etc.

'I take on the suffering of all the denizens of hell.' The bodhichitta absorbs the pain of the hell-beings and releases them.

In the Animal Realm

Use memories of raw fear ('eat or be eaten', 'the law of the jungle') and stupidity, and self-denigrating thoughts, and thoughts of claustrophobic constraint to enter the animal realm of wild or domestic animals. Recognize grey color. Recognize the fear and mindlessness in dualistic perception. Imagine wandering in great fear through the animal realms.

I am a wolf (howl), a lion (roar), a bird (chirrup and sing), a
       rat.
I am the predator stalking, pouncing and killing.
I am the victim, caught, killed, pulled apart and eaten.
I am the beast of burden, contracted to slavery.

I am a dog (whoof, whine), a cat (meow), a pig (oink), a
horse (neigh) etc., etc.

'I take on the suffering of the animals in their wild or
domesticated state in order to release them from that
rebirth.'

In the Human Realm
Use thoughts of insufficiency and the need for
improvement; thoughts of greed and sexual fulfilment, and
memory of human distress and moments of tears to enter
the human realm. Recall moments of absurdity and farce to
instigate laughter. Recognize the lurid color orange.
Recognize the inevitable suffering of embodiment. Focus
on the stages of life in turn. Imagine wandering through the
human realm with compassion.

I am squeezed and pulled in the birth canal, in the agony of
birth.
I am a baby sucking, crawling and mewling.
I am an adolescent suffering growth pains and sexual
trauma.
I am a pregnant woman giving birth.
I am a rich person living in luxury, commanding servants.
I am poor, hungry, neglected, mistreated.
I am sick and weak with incurable disease.
I am an old, bent, with a stick, blind and deaf.
I am senile, stupid and atrophied.
I am the guilt-stricken, culpable sinner.
I am an inadequate, ineffectual loser, etc., etc.

'I take upon myself all human suffering.'

In the Titanic, Demonic, Asura Realm
Use thoughts of envy and jealousy and memories of
paranoid competitive situations to enter the titanic,
demonic realms. Recognize a deep dark verdant green
color. Recognize the innate tendency to inflate oneself and

demean others. Imagine wandering through the demonic realms.

I am a young titan fighting against the old gods.
I am angry at imperfection and denigrate the weak and
      helpless.
I envy the rich and powerful, and fight for the revolution.
I am jealous of my love, paranoiac and resentful.
I am fearful of the environment, always looking over my
      shoulder, etc., etc.

'I take upon myself the envy and paranoia of the titans.'

In the Realm of the Hungry Ghosts
Use lustful thoughts and sexual fantasy to enter the realm of the hungry ghosts. Also, memories of personal addiction and compulsion, Recognize the deep crimson red color. Recognize the tendency to desire food, sex, and goods to compensate for insecurity. Imagine wandering in the realm of the hungry ghosts.

I am a spirit unable to find rest.
I am a junkie unable to find my next fix.
I can't get no satisfaction.
I am lost in frustrated hunger and thirst.
I am constantly lost in self-defeating impotence.
I am always dissatisfied, misery is my lot, etc., etc.

'I take upon myself the pain of impotence of the hungry ghosts.'

In the Realm of the Gods
Use arrogant, proud and conceited thoughts of personal identity, memories of callous, ruthless acts of injustice, and arbitrary use of power to enter the realm of the gods. Recognize the dirty yellow color. Recognize the potential for personality inflation as compensatory mechanism. Imagine wandering through the paradisal realms of the

gods. Recognize the five signs of the god's degeneration: soiled dress, fading garlands, perspiration, foul smell repulsing young gods and goddesses, discomfort while on the throne.

I am Jehovah, Lord of All, a jealous God, protecting my people.
I am a Christ on the Cross, God of Love.
I am the Virgen de Guadalupe,
I am Zeus, Lord of all gods and humans, in total control.
I am Mahadev, the Great God, Lord of All.
I am all-powerful and lustful, performer of miracles.
I am the Mother Goddess, easy to anger, easy to love.
I am the Virgin Goddess, pure and simple.
I am a god/goddess of lubricious, sensory pleasure.
I am a god of aesthetic form taking every experience as perfect in itself, etc., etc.

'I take upon myself the pain of the gods' fear of eventual downfall.'

And, then, finally:
I am Buddha under the bodhi-tree, enlightened. I turn the wheel of dharma. I recite the *Prajnaparamita-sutras*.

See below (p.26) under the heading 'Crucial Endgame: Neduwa' for the consummate finale.

Unstructured Practice

The unstructured or unpremeditated practice can be prefaced by as little or as much of the preliminary ritual as the yogin/yogini feels necessary. But unless the mindstate is customarily fluid and creative, bordering on the unstable, it may be advisable to increase the preparation rather than ignore it.

In general, the principle of unstructured practice is to remove the physical, energetic and mental restraints from karmic proclivity and act out karma without inhibition. In this practice, we have left behind the boxed categories of the wheel of life and rely on more formless and unimaged structure. Not only are the forms of expression more abstract but the movement from one to another is left to the personal subconscious, to lateral association rather than serial connection. The rational controller put aside, illogical, abrupt transition is to be expected. The following notions are not to be taken as a given agenda, but rather as signposts for the will wandering at a loss in the unconscious. This list is an example of one individual's imagination. Use it, but build upon it, delve deep into your own unconscious, and uncover the extent of your own madness.

On the physical plain (body): take off your clothes; exercise facial contortion (Japanese Noh play!); do the hand-jive; develop hand and arm dancing; cultivate extreme postures and contortion, jumping or twisting on the ground; tree-climbing; running in circles; impulsive calisthenics. Take inspiration from the army and from the zoo, from animals, insects and birds. More evidently, perform free-form dance (that has no repetitive theme) and act out formlessly. The 'nine moods of the dakinis' provide moods for such dance: erotic, heroic, disgusting, furious, humorous, frightful, compassionate, wonderful, tranquil are the traditional moods of the dakinis, according to classical Indian calculation.

On the vocal plain, with the voice: speak out your thoughts without design, talk to yourself about the moment without strategy; talk nonsense, gibberish, monkey talk, baby talk; speak your home-made language; talk the pre-speech of your ancestors; copy animal sounds and spirit noises; sing popular songs; artlessly compose and arrange your own songs; sing original opera; chant mantras, nursery rhymes, poetry; rehearse the entire scope of scream; find the primal scream; cry, weep; giggle, laugh, play the fool. Whisper, talk, shout and scream. Talk like a child to children.

On the mental plain, with the mind: sit and let your thoughts run freely; allow the imagination uninhibited play; indulge unconstrained fantasy, give yourself sexual control (and act out wherever possible).

In case of getting stuck, physically fall back upon the vajra standing posture that is included in the inner rushen. This exercise is a surefire method of focus and concentration. Aim at maintaining the posture for ten minutes. With energetic freezing, with a sense of sense of limitation or inhibition, conscientiously scream. With repetitive or constant fatigue chant scripture or poetry.

So long as we controlled by social constraint, so long as social conditioning holds us in its maw, we are unable to let go and break free into the arena of unstructured practice. If we cannot find a crack in the fabric of conditioned response (habit) which we can work into a highway leading to a hive of inventive play, song and dance, then we can fall back upon the social devices that have been employed traditionally to enable us to let go: namely music, dance, and alcohol and psychedelic substances such as cannabis. Regarding music the shaman's drum (and the drum in general) should be high on the list. The mantras of wrathful protectors can also be very effective in breaking down resistance, mantra such as RULU RULU HUNG JO HUNG. The mantras of serenity, such as OM AH HUNG and the Tara mantra TARE TU TARE break down inbred resistance. Retain a sense of the rushen purpose in all situations and at all cost.

If you can enter into this unstructured practice fully, the result will be stronger than that of the formal practice. The acting-out may have been effective in improving your theatrical or communication skills, but the great virtue of the exercise is the loosening and expressing of karmic tendencies hitherto hidden in the 'subconscious'. Sources of irritation are eradicated, and we ride free. The force of the practice and its call upon our energy reserves should be optimized. The practice is not complete until the organism is totally exhausted, straining to refill its lungs with a simple breath, panting like at the end of the chase, or at the point of exhaustion after sexual consummation.

In the excitement of success in equalizing samsara and nirvana, do not forget the neduwa!

If in either the formal or unpremeditated versions of practice the impulse to abandon the rushen overwhelms you, Don't let it! Perseverance furthers! Remember your vow to finish the retreat.

Consider the possibility of combining the formal and unstructured rushen, in each session beginning with the formal structure and later incorporating the unstructured finale.

Crucial Endgame: Neduwa

After the highly energetic action of the central part of the practice, either formal or unstructured, the neduwa tends to get lost as an appended irrelevancy. But on the contrary, everything that has gone before it can be considered preliminary. The neduwa is the rest at the end of dynamic practice, complete repose after exhaustion, after the energy of body, speech and mind has been spent. In that bardo, whether it is an intermission in practice or the final session of the day, lie down exhausted on your right side, like Sakyamuni Buddha on his deathbed, in the complete cathartic relaxation of exhaustion. Here, when the mind is too tired to protect or dissemble, we may watch the nature of mind in all its naked glory. If we fail in this, the karma-production that has been working at full steam will have its head and overwhelm you with the effective concatenation of your mad exposition. So settle freely into the natural state of authenticity, naturalness (*nebab*), allowing karma to eat itself up. This state of relaxation can last between five and fifteen minutes or more.

If in the excitement of success, you feel the urge to share your experience, suppress it. It is unwise to share these precepts or your personal experience until success has become immaterial.

Alternative Rushen: Acting Out Socially

For some people, the practices described above, the formal rushen, and even the unstructured rushen, smack too much of artificial and contrived ritual. For them it may feel more acceptable to find in the flow of life activity that mimics the rushen retreat. If we can find activities with analogous form, then by providing them with rushen motivation and purpose they may fulfil the same function and deliver the same result as our retreat rituals. Can we integrate our khorde rushen practice into everyday life? Probably not – unless in our day-to-day round or in our profession we are engaged in extraordinary activity – the circus comes to mind, any lifestyle that is free of social inhibition. Many vignette activities, however, can be envisioned as Dzogchen yoga, and thus the rushen can be incorporated, occasionally, into the stream of life. These activities include disco or modern dance; formal acting in the theatre or on the street; professional singing on the stage or in the studio. Then sexual activity, casual-spontaneous or premeditated, can also become rushen activity for most of us, provided the rushen motivation is in place. In or out of the bedroom, with an initiated or ignorant but willing partner, sexual interaction can be impregnated with the awareness of khorde rushen. The essential condition, of course, is the neduwa, the built-in neduwa, or failing orgasm a sought for and indulged neduwa at the conclusion of a period of sexual indulgence. Further, pornographic sexual activity can provide an ideal arena in less socially aware occasions. Verbal argument and even physical violence between couples can be utilized when both individuals understand the rushen infrastructure.

In the bedroom we enact the lust of animals and hungry ghosts; on the football pitch (and sometimes driving vehicles) we enact the anger and rage of the hell-realms and of the demonic gods. Surely every day in business and boardroom, in both professional and social roles, the power of the titans and gods comes into play. Martial arts, athletics and common sports develop but only partially sublimate anger and pride, while jealousy is the very stuff of competition. What differentiates such activities realized with awareness from khorde rushen yogas is the neduwa.

All these activities can socialize and to some extent sublimate deeply innate emotional karmic tendencies and of course thereby release repressed personal and social forces. It is the neduwa that must somehow be integrated into life itself if the karmic root of destructive activities is to be eradicated. With the neduwa, the wheel of life is transformed into buddha-fields with the means of liberation; without it, social interaction is given a safety valve but remains essentially egocentric.

Particular kinds of traveling can be turned into natural rushen. In the desert or mountain wastes of Tibet, the traveling yogin, if he so desired, could be certain of finding himself alone at night and sure of finding a solitary place of practice during the day. Although practicing rushen while on the move is an option, to find a country with the necessary space and facility for solitary trekking is nigh impossible today. To make rushen possible while traveling amongst men, we need to retain a space of internal silence. Under that condition the contingencies of the road can replace spontaneous internal reactivity. Food and lodging are no longer issues. Again, don't forget the neduwa.

Signs of Success

Tibetan manuals delight in listing the relative signs of any given practice, but that should not obscure the fact that the primary purpose of Dzogchen practice is to heighten the clarity and light of immediacy, or to prepare the moment for realization of a greater awareness that anyhow has always been present. These physical, verbal and mental considerations, may be the outward evidence of inner realization. But surely they can manifest also as phenomenal indications of illusory transformation.

Physical indications of awareness of the nirmanakaya (*tulku*) are a feeling of disembodiment, lack of a body. Sensation of temperature, hot and cold, may vanish, together with any feeling of hunger and thirst, and sense of fatigue. In any ordinary situation a sense of the lightness of being will arise perhaps with a sensation of flying, and blissful warmth may blaze through the body.

Energetic and verbal signs of the sambhogakaya (*longchoku*) are an involuntary fluency in other languages ('speaking in tongues'), particularly in the universal language (English?). Verbal expression of the truth of Dzogchen will arise artlessly and extemporaneously. Song may well up within us without any apparent cause or purpose. On the other hand, resting in a sense of the ineffable, there may be no desire at all to speak.

Mental indication of the dharmakaya (*choku*) may be described as rainbow light in the sky, as sensory fields of radiance and brilliance, but that is mere poetic license. More explicitly, interpretive and judgmental thought ceases, and even descriptive and appreciative thought is no longer objectified. It is as if the root of the rational mind has been severed. To put it another way perception has become nonconceptual. Further, karmic conditioning has ceased, and with the winding down of affective karma transmigration also ends.

Part Two: Texts and Transcripts

Separating Samsara and Nirvana: The Khorde Rushen

This excerpt from the classical 18ᵗʰ century Dzogchen manual of Jigme Lingpa, the Yeshe Lama, *delineates the practice of rushen according to the lights of the late Tibetan tradition. This form of practice, unfortunately, has fallen into disuse. The next paragraph is a precis of various sources.*

Go to a mountain where neither man nor beast passes: find a solitary place and a comfortable seat to practice on. Take a little water and corn or rice, bless it and throw it into the air offering it to lama, yidam, dakini and protectors, and particularly to the mountain god, shouting 'Lhagyelo'. Request protection from disturbances of man or beast and adventitious obstacles. Make the same offering to the nature spirits, to the elementals, to the local spirits of earth and rocks, saying, 'Take, eat and be happy!' Make an offering of incense to the lotus-eaters and the hungry-ghosts. Take off your clothes and remain naked, without shame or blame.

Train in the exercises that illuminate and purify samsara and nirvana and release us from both.[1] *Beyond the Sound* says,

Without the practice that separates samsara and nirvana
Links with the material triple world[2] remain.

---

[1] Tulku Thondrup consistently translates the phrase *'khor 'das ru shan dbye ba:* as 'exercises that release us from both samsara and nirvana'.

[2] The three realms of samsara (*khams gsum*) are the realms of sensory desire, aesthetic form and formlessness.

Here I teach you the exercises,
Physical, energetic and mental,
That existentially define samsara and nirvana.

These physical, vocal and mental rushen are explained under five headings: purpose, place, the development of enlightened mind inducing the proper attitude, how to practice, and concluding contemplation (the result).

Physical Rushen: Clarifying Samsara

Purpose: The body is a product of ignorance wandering continually lost in samsara. To free ourselves from this condition, we train physically in the exercises that clarify and define samsara experientially. The purpose of these exercises is to liberate ourselves from samsara.

Place: To practice find a quiet mountain valley, or a pleasant solitary place, unfrequented by human beings, where people who may react negatively to our behavior, can neither be seen or heard.

Proper Attitude: Repeat this intention to develop the correct attitude: 'I attain buddha for the sake of all living beings. To that end I train myself physically in the profound exercises that clearly illuminate samsara,[3] thereby releasing me from it, never to return.'

Practice: The *Testament* defines the physical practice like this,

The body is primed through this training:
First, act out the behavior of the six types of beings,
And then imitate the Buddha.

---

[3] *'Khor ba ru shan:* 'that existentially defines samsara precisely'.

Enact the behavior of the six types of beings of the six realms. Act out the suffering from heat and cold of the inhabitants of hell; the hunger and thirst of the hungry ghosts; the slavery of animals; the wars of the demonic demi-gods; the dying and death of the gods; and the birth, old-age, sickness and death of human beings. Enact without shame the behavior of them all, whatever comes to mind, without concern for morality; perform spontaneously, but without preference or bias. Finish one enactment completely before starting a new. Do not leave time between one and the next.

The Result: The signs of completing these exercises are an absence of attachment or craving, hope or doubt, and an even manner in approach to all six emotional states.

Physical Rushen: Clarifying Nirvana

To clarify nirvana, enact the behavior of the peaceful and wrathful buddha-deities. Spontaneously copy their postures and manners – whatever comes to mind. Do not unduly prolong any particular activity; add one to the next without a break. Train in this until desire for any result has dissolved and a state of equanimity has been reached.

Concluding Contemplation: The continual enactment of samsara and nirvana in a theatrical manner finally exhausts our imagination regarding the behavior of the six kinds of being in their mythic realms. Whenever that happens relax naturally and rest in the state of exhaustion. If any further insight into their behavior arises, act it out again and again, until you are certain that the potential is exhausted.

Speech Rushen: Clarifying Samsara

Purpose: The *Testament* has it:

Speech is primed by this training:
Imitate the various sounds of six-realm beings

And then the sounds of the wrathful and peaceful deities,
Both harsh and pleasant sounds.

By grasping and clinging to people's speech, construing it
sometimes as good and sometimes bad, the various karmas
are created that enmesh us in samsara: we need to be free
of those karmas.

Proper Attitude: Repeat this to develop the correct attitude:
'From now on, for the sake of all living beings, I shall
practice these methods that prevent my speech from
straying into samsara.'

The place: Go to a place where no other people go.

The practice: Shriek 'ouwah!' for the pain, 'gahh!' for the
burning and 'aargh!' for the misery of the abyss.[4] Screech
out in hunger and thirst like the hungry ghosts. Imitate the
unintelligible sounds of animals, such as 'groar!' and
'meuw!; the howls of 'eat!' and 'kill!' of the demonic demi-
gods; and purr in the satisfaction and enjoyment of the
gods. Shout out in one's own or others' languages the
sounds of pleasure attained. Recall and give voice to your
response to the lies and slander that you have endured.
Swear and curse at the top of your lungs again and again.
Then abruptly terminate it as above.

Speech Rushen: Clarifying Nirvana

The sound of nirvana is heard in many and various ways:
in the sixty melodies of the peaceful buddha-deities, in the
eighteen laughs of the wrathful buddha-deities, and in the
various sounds of the elements, for example. Imitate
whatever of their sounds comes to mind. As the sign of
accomplishment, true realization of all the lamas' verbal
teaching arises in thought, and words of truth will

---

[4] In Tibetan: *ana!*, *atsa!* and *kye hud!*

suddenly burst out of us. Train in the rushen of speech until such accomplishment is experienced.

Concluding contemplation: At the end of each period of training, relaxing in the mindstream in the place where nondiscrimination between good and bad sounds or words, is found, stay in that place and relax naturally. Discover when such experience takes place in the mindstream.

Mental Rushen: Defining Samsara

The purpose: the relative mind – the intellect – is inseparable from the enlightened-mind of buddha, yet due to a lack of recognition of the mind's nature, we are caught in samsara. The purpose of the mental rushen is to bring release to the relative mind.

Proper Attitude: Develop enlightened mind by thinking, 'So that I may attain buddha for the benefit of all living beings, so that all beings cease their wandering in samsara, I commit myself henceforth to this training.'

Habitation: To practice the mental rushen, we should go to a solitary place. The *Testament* advises,

Mind is primed by this training:
Suffer the pain of the six realms.

Practice: Imagine the suffering of heat and cold in the hell realms; the suffering of hunger and thirst of the hungry ghosts; the suffering of domestic slavery and the eat-or-be-eaten panic of the animals; the suffering of constant conflict of the demonic demi-gods; the suffering of distraction and thought of inevitable downfall of the gods; and the various sufferings of birth, aging, sickness and death of human beings. Imagine it and intimately experience it. When one train of thought ends, immediately begin another. Develop such thinking forcefully and terminate it abruptly.

Concluding contemplation: When the mind remains in a non-arising state, stay in that place of contemplation. Notice when contemplation consumes the mindstream.

Mental Rushen: Defining Nirvana

Purpose, Place and Attitude: The information under these headings is similar to those of the section on mental exercises providing release from samsara.

Practice: Think of a pure-land as high as Mt. Sumeru. Here, the pure-land of manifest joy is in the east; the pure-land of virtuous array is in the south; the pure-land of great bliss is in the west; and the pure-land of the perfection of sublime activity is in the north. The pure-lands of the bodhisattvas are in the four intermediate directions and the extra-ordinary pure-lands of emanation are at the zenith and the nadir. At the apex is the unexcelled pure-land of spacious-ness. Buddhas with their hosts of companions are the actual beings dwelling in all these pure-lands. Think in that way repeatedly and then terminate thought.

Concluding Contemplation: Finding a space in which no concepts arise, stay there in natural ease. Notice whether nonconceptual experience is happening in the mindstream.

Through such training, mental obscuration dissolves; mental obstructions vanish; intractable perceptions are released; and the realization of inseparability from the mind of buddha is actualized in attainment of buddha.

These rushen exercises release us physically, energetically and mentally from the cause and effect dilemmas of samsara and from identity with its positive and negative extremes; thereby, physical, energetic and mental grasping at the phenomena of nirvana through concepts' tight grip is released. This is the most excellent method of welcoming actual realization.

Our physical, energetic and mental functions are tangled up in the complexities of samsara and nirvana. The superior way of disentangling them is through the physical, energetic and mental rushen in which we act out our behavior in both samsara and nirvana. It is said,

Concepts refine concepts,
Phenomena cleanse phenomena,
Just as water caught in the ear
Is released by an injection of water.

The last-resort method of releasing water caught in the ear is to inject more water. Similarly, we can abandon the rigid concepts that make us cling to the activities of samsara and nirvana by bringing them out into the open. By mimicking the behavior caused by immersion in samsara and nirvana, our thoughts are loosened and freed.

If we neglect these three rushen exercises, the *Secret Lamp of Crucial Instruction* warns, 'If we omit these rushen exercises defining and thus releasing us from samsara and nirvana, we tend to feel like unescorted travelers in dangerous or unknown places.'

The Methods of Relaxing the Three Doors

After finishing whatever physical exercise is being undertaken, cease all activity whatsoever. Sit down on a comfortable seat and relax naturally in contemplation. That is relaxation of body. Relaxation of speech is to remain silent, making neither words nor sounds. Relaxation of mind is to act as if totally exhausted.

When body, speech and mind are relaxed, notice the difference between the state of hazy thinking that characterized the releasing exercises and the present state of mind that is so relaxed and quite spent. Where lies the most thinking? Which state is the stronger and which more stable?

In the *Secret Lamp of Crucial Instruction*, it is said, 'During relaxation meditation, feel your body as light and insubstantial as a cloud, as mist or as cotton flowers. When an impulse to speak arises, seal it with the unborn syllable 'A'. During mental relaxation, it is crucial that your meditation is as unmoving as an iron castle.'

Settling into the natural state, thinking nothing, remain in it for as long as possible, but if thoughts do arise adventitiously, use these relaxation meditations as their antidotes.

The benefits of these relaxation meditations are mentioned in *Radiant Awareness*:

Relaxation of the body provides a certain boost to the body, the constitution and the senses, and an increase in seed-essence (semen, bodhichitta). Relaxation of speech brings realization of unfabricated and inexpressible reality and exhausts verbal analysis. Mental relaxation frees us from obsessive mental attachments.

If we neglect this training in the three aspects of relaxation, The *Secret Lamp of Crucial Instruction* warns, 'If you lack these three types of relaxation, you face exhaustion, like someone who has labored for days and nights without sleeping.'

Khorde Rushen
Direct Introduction to Pure Presence

The Lamrim Yeshe Nyingpo *followed the* Yeshe Lama, *its root and precursor,* exceeding it in clarity and precision. *The root text is a concise mind-terma of Chokgyur Lingpa and Jamyang Khyentse Wangpo, but the commentary included here was written by Jamgon Kongtrul, done in the 19ᵗʰ century.*

The tantra the *Only Son of the Teaching* advises,

Initially, to slacken the fixations
Of body, speech and mind
Start with behavior,
The rushen of body

How to practice the rushen of body is explained in the root tantra:

With the body in motion or reclining,
twisting and turning, perform yoga postures,
Stretch and bend the limbs
And put the body through its paces.
Just as you conceive it, physically enact
The behavior of the six types of beings.

Accordingly, in order to revert the physical, vocal and mental activity initiated by karma and natural propensity, and in the future to halt it entirely, go to a place where it is certain that no one will intrude and where you cannot be seen or heard so that you will not breach the seventh root-downfall that deals with concealing secret conduct.

In that place make torma offerings to the local landlord spirits, entreating their indulgence for your unconventional behavior, requesting them to refrain from jealous suspicion. Then say to yourself, 'I am here for the sake of all sentient beings to separate, distinguish and define samsara and nirvana physically, energetically and mentally so that in the future I need not return to samsara.'

The Rushen of Body

After generating bodhi-mind in that way, strip naked and imagine and act out successively the extreme heat and cold of the denizens of hell, the hunger and thirst of the hungry ghosts, the slavery of the animals, the birth, old age sickness and death of human beings, the war and strife of the demonic anti-gods, and the inevitable fall of the gods.[5]

Then, run and jump, twist and turn, stretch and bend and, in brief, move your body in whatever comes to mind – but without purpose or design.

Rushen of Speech

Then, similarly, in order to pull apart and define samsara and nirvana in speech, *Beyond the Sound* instructs:

So that we need not mock anything we hear,
Speak - indiscriminately - the languages
Of the gods, serpents, nature spirits
Lotus eaters, young siren singers and lordly men.[6]

In brief, speak the languages of the six types of beings – However they come to mind. Chatter nonsensically to yourself and speak various languages randomly.

---

[5] The khorde rushen is particularly suited to 'the diligent person fond of courageous conduct', *Light of Wisdom* p.93. The extrovert naturally manifests the khorde rushen; the introvert needs application.

[6] *Devas, nagas, yakshas; gandharvas, kimbhandhas* and *narayanas.*

Rushen of Mind

Then, again, to separate samsara and nirvana in mental activity, the *Heir of Buddha* instructs,

Think about joy and sorrow, pleasure and pain,
Permanence and impermanence for example;
Think about view, meditation and action
And what dharma is and is not and so forth;
Think about desire, anger and stupidity
And virtue and vice and all manner of topics.

Consciously and forcefully provoke both positive and negative thoughts about past, present and future, letting them rise and fall. Eventually, you will be physically, energetically and mentally exhausted, and looking at the place where intellectual arrogance is deflated, totally relax.

Again, it is said in the *Last Testament*, 'Also specifically enact buddhist practice.'

Assume the meditation posture with legs crossed and the earth-touching mudra; project and absorb rays of light from the urna;[7] imagine wearing lama's robes; and eyes lowered, focus them an arm's length to the front: all peaceful disciplined conduct. The activity of buddha-speech is recitation of the sutras such as the Heart Sutra and the parroting of analytical formulae and Middle Way (Consequence)[8] refutation.

Then, assume wrathful postures and the nine dramatic expressions[9] and articulate their verbal corollaries.

---

[7] The point between the eyebrows marked in the buddha by a coiled hair.

[8] *Madhyamika-prasangika (Dbu ma thal 'gyur).*

[9] The nine moods of dance (*gar dgu*) derived from the Indian tradition: erotic, heroic, disgusting, furious, humorous, frightful, compassionate, wonderful, tranquil.

enunciating RULU RULU, HUNG HUNG and PHAT PHAT for example, thus developing proficiency in expression of many different moods. As the *Last Testament* says:

Articulate variously the sounds of dharma –
Mantra and daily recitations,
And the rhetoric of debate and discussion,
Existence, nonexistence and luminosity.

In the above exposition the divisions and existential definitions of samsara and nirvana is practiced through the separate activity of body, speech and mind, which is the usual manner in basic training. But when the separation and definition of samsara and nirvana is practiced with body, speech and mind simultaneously, in every configuration of unitary samsara and nirvana, body, speech and mind will arise naturally as the play of buddha-body, speech and mind.[10]

Engaging diligently in this rushen practice for a fortnight, eleven days or even a week,[11] physical, energetic and mental fixation in the moment will be alleviated by itself and the connection to samsara will be permanently interrupted.

Ultimately, boundless benefits will accrue: the body will mature as clear light, speech will be clarified as circles of letters;[12] and mind will be released as pure presence. In short, as it is said in *Understanding Empowerment,*

---

[10] This statement elevates khorde rushen to a very high level of practice. It also implies that separation of samsara and nirvana allows them to snap back into a natural unitary mold.

[11] These periods of practice are minimal; three months or more was common in Tibet.

[12] Arising spontaneously without hesitation in the manner of the syllables of a mantric circle appearing involuntarily in the mind's eye (*yi ge 'khor lo*).

Whoever practices the rushen
Does not return to the triple world.[13]

---

[13] The triple world (*khams gsum*) consists of the realms of desire (*'dod pa'i khams*), form or aesthesis (*gzugs khams*), and formlessness (*gzugs med kyi khams*).

Bollschweil: Rushen Retreat

This is part of the transcript of a talk given to a group of German practitioners very early in their practice. It provides the rationale and the instruction for elementary or simple khorde rushen.

This rushen practice is to a large degree about mental focus, focusing the relative mind. The way it's said in the old texts is 'separating samsara from nirvana'. We all know the meaning of samsara and nirvana. Samsara in Tibetan (*khorwa*) means 'the round', 'the cycle'. What round? It indicates a series of moments or lifetimes in a wheel of time. This implies transmigration from existence in one mental state to another, from one realm of existence to another. That's samsara, and when the wheel turns faster than the mind can conceive, samsara is confusion and ignorance. Nirvana, simply put, is freedom from that revolving wheel. It is a peaceful place with clarity, a place of unlimited spaciousness, cognition of emptiness, and consequent detachment.

Samsara and nirvana in this frame form a duality; but then there is the great nirvana, mahanirvana, which is the union of these two things. So please understand that nirvana is not Dzogchen; it's not the Dzogchen state. Nirvana here is the absence of samsara.

This khorde rushen practice is concerned with clarifying this samsara – and nirvana also. Consider the mirror for a moment – the mirror is a potent symbol in the Dzogchen view. The mirror itself symbolizes the nature of mind and whatever appears in the mirror are the forms of mind. Whether it's action of body, speech or mind, whatever arises in the nature of mind is what we are focusing upon

here in the khorde rushen, and focusing on it we name it,
categorize it, and make clear the scope of it and the quality
of it.

The blueprint that we use to separate, isolate and identify
aspects of the mind and the dominant emotions are the six
realms of the wheel of life. This, as you very well know, is
composed of the realms of the gods and the demonic anti-
gods, the human realm - these three comprise the upper
realms - and then the animal realm, the realm of the pretas
- the hungry ghosts - and the hell-realms comprise the
lower realms. These six 'realms', this tabulation,
encompasses all our potential, in terms of emotion and
confusion and varying mindstates. We can stretch the limits
of the realms, or find the cusps between them, in order to
identify the intermediate spaces where the various
emotions are mixed up. In order to define, to focus and
define, our various emotions, in order to know who we are,
and what we are made of, we can see all experience
reflected in these six realms of the wheel of life. If we want
to know what is going on in our mind, look into the
mirrorlike wheel of life and identify and label what we find
accordingly.

Identify the reflections in the mirror in order to practice our
basic Dzogchen meditation of watching the mind, using the
contents of the mind as the doors to the nature of mind (the
state of Samantabhadra). To use the contents as doors to the
state of contemplation we need to be able to identify them
clearly. We need to be able to see what's arising in the
mirror. If we've got only a blur, a smear of totally chaotic
elements in the mirror, we are not focused and we are not
meditating. We're not even able to start Dzogchen practice.
This rushen is a process of discrimination (a prelude to
Dzogchen 'nondiscrimination'). In this process of
discrimination, we use body, speech and mind, and this
basic practice can be best described as 'acting out'. We need
to bring up from the depths of the mind the potential for

experience in the six realms, so that we can identify them and focus them, recognizing our varying mindstates.

This function of opening up subconscious areas of the mind so that their contents become apparent, is not specific to Dzogchen, but the identification with the light of the mind in terms of the six realms is definitely specifically Dzogchen. The motivation, the intent, is crucially Dzogchen. When the contents of the mind are released into our sphere of meditation, we apply exactly the same process of basic Dzogchen (non)meditation that we learnt in the initiatory experience – watching without acceptance or rejection of whatever arises. The result of this practice will be more fluidity in the mind, a broader, wider, scope of activity in the mind, more movement, change, feeling, included, the whole gamut of the wheel of life fully recognized and assimilated.

It's an unhealthy mind that is closed, suppressed and unknowing – by definition it is 'ignorant'. The rushen enlightens it. We do it by acting-out ordinary social roles, social roles indicated by the six realms of the wheel of life. Identify with one of the six realms, enact it theatrically in solitude and our karma in that realm is reduced or perhaps consumed. Somebody, for example, plays the god in power manipulation. He imagines the form of the god, the mudra of the god, and mimics the vocal tones of the god. He plays the function of the god, through manipulation. This is not necessarily minor social power-tripping, perhaps he sits on the top of a giant corporation, or on throne in a gompa or a church or whatever, ordering the mandala surrounding him, and fully playing out this persona. Or, the demonic anti-god, the titan: here is the revolutionary, the insurgent, the rebel constantly trying to undermine the guy with the control, the guy who is sitting on top of him. Or the social animal is the one with teeth who never stops showing them in order to feed his greed. The preta, the hungry ghost, may look like the selfish giant, deserving of pity, a a sorry mess, but beware of the locked-up power. Likewise, the hell-being is a dangerous mix of the devil who tortures and the tortured victim.

Act it out! Magnify ordinary social roles. Nothing here is specific to Tibet, or to buddhism. Enact your wheel of life!

Simontornya: Rushen Retreat

This talk was the first given in Simontornya, Hungary, as instruction and inspiration for a ten-day khorde rushen retreat in a thick forest. Most participants had already had some previous experience of rushen, so some of the exposition in this first talk of the retreat is sketchy. The inspirational aspect sometimes involves less than strict Dzogchen argument and metaphor. No distinction is made here between instruction for men and women except where it is made explicit.

I'm going to dive straight into the rushen. First some theory, or better, the view. But don't for an instant think that this view – the theoretical part, the intellectual understanding – is what we're here for. This khorde rushen is fundamentally existential, experiential. And I want to explain how that is and why that is, and then you'll be fully engaged in the plot.

We start with the assumption that we are messed up, which is one way of saying that we are embodied and that our karmas are complex. We have a body, this entity that we inhabit, that has its own rhythms, its own imperatives, its own priorities. Those priorities – simply stated – are survival and reproduction, and under those headings we may subsume virtually everything that we do in this lifetime. In order that we should survive and reproduce, we manufacture chemicals in our body that work for emotions, primarily anger and desire. We need the anger to protect ourselves and our families, our children, and to accept some things and to reject other things, so that we can live in a well-organized community. As for desire, of course desire is primarily to reproduce, but that fundamental sexual urge, the lust, is rechanneled, so we get desire for food, alcohol, comestibles, for a house, a car, to get the status and the luxuries that make life easier and more comfortable. Life is bound up with desire and reproduction.

So let us begin with the basic recognition of the body-mind as a vehicle for survival and reproduction. Get rid of the idea of the fallen angel. We may be a variety of being that holds the potential for transformation, recognition of ourselves as something other than an organic machine for eating and copulating, but the starting point, the taking off point, is recognition of ourselves as human beings. If anyone has a notion that what we're doing here is something other than recognition of that humanity, recognition of our existential imperative for survival and reproduction, that we are actually something divine, transcendental, or, anyway, a being that can escape its body into an Aladdin's cave of the mind, then let's discuss it now, because this body-mind is the base and we have to be clear about it.

The downside of accepting our human nature is that anger and desire – all emotion – is painful. Seeing ourselves as vessels of these emotions we must acknowledge that they are very difficult to carry, difficult to handle. The gnarly grit of hatred and lust makes us lose the thread, lose the page, and forgetting what the main thing is, we go into excess in different ways. I'm not talking about fighting and fucking, I'm pointing at the tendency, the habit, of turning the sexual desire that is built into the body for reproduction into a means of pleasure, a method of substitute satisfaction, sublimation into social etiquette or large bank balance or business performance. Turning aggression into a football match is sublimation.

We live in a state of confusion, and human beings have developed various ways to deal with it. The monastery is one way that chemical effect is reduced to a very minimum. Repression keeps the karma in check, and when karma is dealable then some satisfaction may arise. The monastery was king in Europe for many hundreds of years and in Asia likewise, particularly of course in Tibet. Monasticism gave way to idealization of the extended household, and then to feed the capitalists to the secularized single-family household with its rules and repressions, with its rigid conventions and sad limitations, with its social sham, its falsities.

A third way, fallen into disrepute in the West, sometimes persecuted, is that of the independent religious, the yogin, the sadhu. All yogins are not ascetic renunciates, although in India that is mainly true, and when I say 'yogin', ladies, the yogini is included. Not all yogins operate outside society, but under this definition all of them make pure awareness the ultimate aim, the reason for being. Those yogins, wherever they live these days, receive a lot of negative feedback from society, because the yogin's way implies breaking social convention. It is a very extreme reaction to the suffering of existence.

Then there's Dzogchen. Dzogchen is the ultimate, uncompromising, middle way. Here nothing is rejected and nothing is cultivated. Let's call it 'ultimate acceptance' and that is the Dzogchen view. The Dzogchen view maintains that whatever eventuates in human experience, right here and now, is perfect in itself. What does that mean? How can that be when we maintain that all human experience is suffering? All experience on the surface is indeed suffering. But the *nature* of mind, the *essence* of the suffering is light and bliss.

All our experience is derived from the five senses, and the incoming sensory information is processed by the mind. And consequent upon that processing we get thought and feeling, emotion and other internal mental phenomena. The five senses plus the emotional, thinking and noumenal functions provide eight inherent consciousnesses. Each of the eight senses, internal and external, has a consciousness attached. That consciousness is a mechanical thing that lights up when an object hits the sense-organ. It is ephemeral, just momentary; so what we call 'consciousness' is momentary series of sensory impressions gathered from all the sensory fields. But in that consciousness, in that *very* consciousness, the light of the mind shines. We identify that light as *rigpa,* a seminal Dzogchen word. It's Awareness. It's present awareness, awareness of the here and now. And it's known only momentarily. It's that Awareness that is the heart of Dzogchen, the great perfection – the nature of mind, in fact. In other words, in every sensory impression, in every experience of the twenty-four hours, we have that light of the mind present. We can't separate it out; it's not something that can be scientifically analyzed and experimented upon. It's not the light of the sun, which is photons or electrons or whatever. It's the light which is there in the mental darkness. Shut yourself up in a dark room and there is still light in the mind, isn't there? It's this mind-light that is the starting point of Dzogchen. It's recognition of that light, that reality, that makes Dzogchen 'experiential'. It transcends all feeling, it transcends all thought.

Now consider the implications of *rigpa*: if it transcends thought, it transcends everything that we think, speak or do. It transcends the sensory process involving subject and object and the interrelationship of the two. Isn't that why we're here today: we have recognized this ground of being, the common basis of humanity. The intellect will question that, because doubting is what the intellect does; that anyway is one of its main functions. What is important, then, is that we are confident in the reality of the light of the mind, in *rigpa*, in that basic awareness, in the spacious awareness that underlies all human experience. When somebody talks about the secret of Tibetan Buddhism, that's it.

Now, we can shout it out, we can infest the media with our knowledge of *rigpa*, but that's not going to make it less secret. Why? Because we can't show it, we can't demonstrate it. We can't even know that we have experienced it. It's the nondual *nature* of being, the ground of being. In mahayana buddhism it is called emptiness – it's nothing, but it's everything.

The intuitive knowing of the *rigpa* is crucial to the practice of khorde rushen. What militates against *rigpa*, what *rigpa* consumes, what the intellect can convince us of, is the fact of karmic cause and effect. 'Karma' is 'action', karma is habit, karma is what we do, and the dynamic behind karma is that we do what we do do because we've done it repeatedly before. The theory of karma is not universally accepted. Look at the history of the 20th century, look at Stalin and Marxism, or look at Hitler's fascism, and what we find is an attempt to impose new patterns of thought and action on entire human societies. It could be said that the attempt to impose ways of thinking and acting was the main political issue in the twentieth century: the truth of karma was ignored or forgotten. This loss implied a new intellectual arrogance, and implicit in it was the certainty that an alien system of belief could be imposed upon the human mind. Well, perhaps those political systems were not total failures, but indeed they didn't work. Ignore the principle of karma at your peril! Ignore the innate tendencies of karma in your mind, in the communal mind, try and over-awe karma with reason and stymie age-old habit patterns and confusion is the result. New moral systems cannot be imposed on the human mind through legislation, by law. The failure of Communism and Fascism is not our only example. What about Christianity? Two thousand years of trying and they're still not off the ground. Consider the Ten Commandments which go back, I don't know, thirty-five hundred years. It's as if they were attacking something really deep in human being. Embodiment itself implies karma antithetical to the Ten Commandments. We're still committing adultery and killing and stealing and lying to the same extent as we were three thousand years ago, aren't we? Has there been any improvement?

So karma is the issue here. Karma is habit, the habit of being in a body, the habit of identifying with the self, and acting out human reaction patterns. Surviving and copulating, all the way down to smoking, drinking, and drug addiction – it's all karmically determined. The unique key Dzogchen adds in response to this apparent karmic imprisonment is what is called 'nonaction'. What we need to do is to realize what is happening when it is happening – that's 'nonaction'. Understand that we don't want to change karma – we don't have to change anything. What we need to do is recognize it for what it is. And that's really the whole story. If we recognize this very moment for what it is, whatever it is, if we're fully in the moment of cognition of sensory perception, we're directly cognizing the internalized vision and identifying with the nondual dimension of light. That three-fold distinction – when we are fully aware of the moment – is applicable to every moment of our existence, twenty-four hours a day, 365 days of the year and for our entire lifetime.

Recognizing that there is nothing to do, nothing that we *can* do; each moment of perception is complete in itself. We can't add anything, we can't subtract anything to make it better. In its *nature* it is light. In its *nature* it is light. And that's the underpinning of our practice. If we understand that; and we *do* understand that, because that's the basic revelation of initiatory experience and the root of experiential Dzogchen, if and when we have basic recognition of the nature of mind, then there's nothing at all that we can do or think or feel, that does not give that light. And with that light comes the clarity and we get the compassion and we get the freedom. Every momentary experience whatsoever provides it. We don't have to close down in a bubble and enter a state of passivity and non-thought; that's something else, that's nothing to do with Dzogchen. Or rather, that state is just another state of being which is included in Dzogchen experience.

So, where're we going with this here? In our ordinary blinkered lives we have something like five degrees of the entire three hundred and sixty degrees of potential experience open to us. We're bound by fear, by social convention, by dualistic morality. We fear the loosening of the demons within us, fear of the dark side. We fear the ghosts that populate our minds. And we fear the purity, by which I mean the dazzling light. That blinkered, fearful half-life is the condition required for doing the householder, the mahayana, bodhisattvic path, or more particularly, if we are walking the path of christian morality.

Initiatory experience of the nature of mind provides the view that releases us into the 360 degrees of Dzogchen potential, that provides us with the view, the Dzogchen view. That nondual view is the ground that supports our practice. If anybody is deceived by doubt, let's work it out. We've got a meeting every morning, and that's when we can cut down the intellectual objections and revert to the experiential.

OK, now I'm going to talk about the practice. First, the seat: we start every session by sitting on it. Start with the Dzogchen ritual, the nine breaths and then the refuge and the intent. Don't ignore the refuge – it's important. And the celebration; that speaks for itself. These are ritual reminders of the basic unvarnished existential fact of being, which is the nature of mind, the light of the mind. Thereafter, perhaps the preliminary exercises, the HUNG breathing, which gets us to the same place – the light of the mind – but through a rather more complicated, complex visualization of energy – through energy. Then the clarification of mind, which leads directly, immediately, to the nature of mind. All the components of this ritual are designed to put us back into that place of recognition of the nature mind. The ritual focus on the nature of mind, brings all our energy back onto our seat and the ritual has created a mandala.

The mandala in this context has two aspects: one is a circle, a protective circle to keep us in and to keep unwanted visitors out, and the other is the boundless expanse, the boundless Dzogchen mandala, the all-inclusive mandala. Don't take the word 'boundless' lightly, because naturally, through our karma, we have made serious exclusions from our mind-mandala. Habitually, we exclude everything that we don't like, particularly people, people we don't allow, who we don't recognize – they're over there somewhere outside, with a gender, race or personality type that we exclude. This Dzogchen mandala is all inclusive, without exception, from top to bottom, excluding nobody; we make no discrimination, no judgement: total tolerance. That's the nature of the basic mandala. Then, when we've got that boundless mandala in place, we can do the khorde rushen. The khorde rushen is acting out all mental states, all the different possibilities that exist in that mandala, or rather, more specifically, all the possibilities of the wheel of life. It's easy enough just to enact our own superficial karma, we sit there and do whatever comes into the mind, reactively. But more than that, the khorde rushen is about acting out hidden aspects of ourselves, which we may call the personalities of others. We enact the personalities of those whom we have excluded – for example, the hungry ghost. We all have hungry ghosts lurking somewhere in inside us, and those personalities are projected outside on people of our acquaintance. The hungry ghost, for example, is projected upon people we know, upon the junkie, whose activity arising out of his habit affects us; upon the sexual predator who is always on our case, always intruding and interfering. Here we have the label we need to act out that personality. The Tibetan wheel of life gives us the archetypes, which are the points of reference we need to catch certain behaviors, vocal and active.

You all know the wheel of life. It's key to this practice; it's a representational point of reference. Keep it in mind. It's so easy to close down during this practice. Relax, take advantage of the total absence of any pressure.

It's the labels that provide the keys, the initial keys for actually doing the khorde rushen. So I'll go through the six basic personality types of the wheel of life, to remind you

The first personality type is represented by the gods in the realm of the gods. There are three basic types of gods. The first, which will ring true for most of us, is the uninhibited sensual type. We find this archetype among the old Greek god of Olympus, the classical gods who were obsessed with power and its selfish usage. In the sexual sphere this manifested as lascivious, uninhibited sexual activity. Power over others, control over them, resulted in their enslavement. Power and control was the mode.

The second level of divine power derives from aesthetic appreciation. This category includes the divine mind of mathematical comprehension and technological savvy. It includes the kind of mind that understands what is going on in a computer, for example, or the mind of musical composition, or the creative mind of fine art, or the mind of natural appreciation.

Maybe I'm not giving that mind a high enough status because only just above it, on the third level of divinity, is the sphere of essences. Here lie the gods of pure consciousness, the gods of love, the gods of space-time. Here are the great gods of the People of the Book: the Jews, Christians and Mohamedans; Brahma, Vishnu and Shiva and the great gods whose names have been lost in hoary time. It's not easy to identify with these gods: the Hindus recommend *samadhi*, *bhakti* and *yoga*. The alchemists, Amerindians, Shaivites and others recommend psychedelics. How do we act out identity in this realm? We need profound imagination here.

The second of the upper realms belongs to the demonic anti-gods. These titans fight the gods for their power. There are two categories here: those who are waiting to usurp the gods and those who have just fallen from the heights of divinity: the young and ambitious and the old and dying. This is the realm of contention and rivalry, the place of constant competition. We find this place in the military, but we also find it in business; and we can find it everywhere. It is very easy to find seeds of it inside ourselves: look for envy and jealousy. Jealousy is the better word where it is synonymous with overpossessiveness. The demonic antigods are in constant war with the gods; but the gods are 'the owners', and they protect what they have. Sometimes the demons win, but usually it's the gods who have the ascendancy. The problem with the demons and the titans is their Achilles heel – a fundamental paranoia. The paranoia impels them to look over their shoulders, which gives their opponents the moment to step up for the crucial murderous blow that loses them the battle and the war. We can make up our own story. To a large extent this khorde rushen is about defining these archetypical personalities. If we can define it, then we can be it and do it ritually.

Then the human realm, the third of the upper realms. This is the realm of moderation; it's the realm of tears and laughter; it's the realm of the pain of birth, of growth and development, adolescence, mating, parenting, and then old age and death. Sickness, I am not forgetting sickness, which can appear at any moment throughout. You can stay in the human realm for the whole of the rushen retreat if you like, but then you are losing the opportunity for exploring the extremities of human possibility.

One of the possibilities that no one should reject is the animal realm. The animal realm is part of the lower realms. It's easy to acknowledge, to identify with, that animal nature, which is very close to us in the evolutionary process. Surely we can find traces of it in the human character. It's always there. We can point at the Nazi SS, again, but we know that they had no monopoly of animal characteristics, which are everywhere; we don't have to look far. The great fear lies in 'kill or be killed' and 'survival of the fittest'. We have two kinds of animals, though, jungle animals that are always ready to kill and domesticated animals stuck in their animal nature but having ransomed their lives through contractual obligation with the superior species – human beings. The latter is a contract with the devil, of course. Animals give their service or body in return for protection. The same kind of deal works for sex workers all the way up to trade-unionists. The animal realm is a very easy one to start with in the rushen practice – all we have to do is to go on all fours and make weird sounds.

Then there's the hell realms. Again, we express the hell realms vocally. The intensity of pain of the vast array of hell realms is determined by the degree of alienation. Alienation from God, or the gods, alienation from the community, alienation from oneself. The feeling of self, the ego is reduced to a tight ball, like an imploding star. This is where the greatest pain on the wheel of life is experienced. This is the place of the primal scream. I hope to hear lots of that in your practice. The hell realms are actually described in the buddhist religion in great detail, highly complex, in varying degrees, out-doing Dante.

Then the hungry ghosts. The realm of the hungry ghosts, of course, is the realm of unfettered desire. I've already used that phrase, to describe the ground of the heavens, but here in the lower realms unfettered desire is frustrated because it's too much to handle, and for that reason it always trips itself up. This is the realm of addiction, where the habit of desire, the habit of greed, becomes overwhelming, obsessional, the only important thing in life. That can certainly be sexual, but surely the shopping malls are full of hungry ghosts. It's consumerism, of course, which is socially accepted. But there are areas of consumerism which are not socially acceptable, particularly drugs, which these days includes tobacco. Here's the classical depiction of the hungry ghost (each of the six archetypes has a physical representation). The hungry ghosts are giants, most of them. Some of them visible, some of them invisible. Giants with gigantic bellies, spindly limbs, arms and legs, gigantic bellies, needle-thin necks, bloated heads, mouths with blazing tongues. Ugly. As ugly as can be. They are cousins of the trolls. (Do you have trolls in your country?) But the hungry ghosts live in the desert. It's always a desert. In the desert they can't find anything to eat or drink. If in the morning they find a drop of dew, then their flaming tongues evaporate it. Or if they find a fragment of food, again, it's toasted, incinerated. Anyway, they can't swallow anything; it can't penetrate their needle thin necks. Even if it were to get into the belly, it would be lost in the vast expanse. Hungry ghosts, incidentally, are direfully afraid of each other.

So there are our six archetypal realms. If, personally, you can find any others, add them to the six.

Practically speaking, and this is the rushen practice that I'm describing now, we're sitting on our seat, we've finished our ritual, and we're going into the wheel of life and taking one of these six realms, whichever one attracts us, and work at it in our minds imaginatively, just how it is. And then we express it vocally. OK? Now we are expressing the six realms vocally. Focusing on each in turn, the easy way to do it is to sing it, or shout it. It doesn't have to make any sense. Make sounds that represent the nature of each realm. The sounds of the animals present no problems, that's clear. Then we've got the primal scream of the hell realms. But, what are the sounds of the hungry ghosts? Sighing and groaning? Wheezing and crying? Not so difficult. And then the sounds of the gods and the demons – that needs some work. Human birth, we say, is characterized by tears and laughter. But in the human realm we have all kinds of options. For starters, we've got the alphabet – the sounds that articulate the alphabet: A-B-C-D-E-F-G. Like that. Then we've got childish chatter, baby talk. We've got the hymns that we learned as children. Or if we didn't learn hymns then nursery rimes. Beatles songs. Folk songs. Opera. There are infinite possibilities of expressing the human realm, vocally.

We can do that vocalization sitting on our seats or we can do it moving around. If we use the latter mode then we're uniting the energetic, 'speech' rushen with the active, physical rushen. Perhaps the easiest way to move into the physical rushen is to dance. First, move in slow-mo with the hands, include the body; stand up and speed up; and we're dancing the six kinds of beings of the wheel of life. Here again, even more here, we need to use our imagination. From here we can go anywhere and do anything. Maybe it's climbing a tree or standing on your head. Try burying your head in the sand! But it's dance. That is the conventional method of expression. Bring the disco into your rushen area and let go. You can do what you will here. With body, speech and mind. The body is dance, the speech is sound, the vocal expression, and the mind is the thought, the analytical, imaginative invocation of a particular archetype.

Now don't get hung up on that praxis, in the actual enactment, in the drama of it. Remember the view – remembrance of the view is the point of it. The purpose of the enactment of body, speech and mind is to prove – to show – that its nature is light, and that we are aware of whatever comes down, whatever archetype is dominant, is light, that we are there and aware of it. That's the entire point of it. Don't lose sight of that – it is liberating. Now, we know that each of the realms – experience of the realms – is transitory. We might say that the gods live forever, but even the gods finally die. And so with the demons. We survive addiction (or some people do). People do come out of the hell realms. Animals have short lives.

We can see that these states that we have been acting-out are just temporary, but only insofar as our awareness of them dominates are we free of them. In so far as we are aware of it, the short moment of our transitory experience appears and then it's gone: awareness consumes karmic effect. And to prove that, to punctuate the practice with that understanding we do the 'neduwa'. This is absolutely essential in the practice, but tangential to the main practice. After each session of practice, we fall into total relaxation. It's like dancing until you drop. When you are exhausted, literally, throw yourself on the ground. There is complete relaxation. At that moment we have the possibility of an unadulterated, unmasked, hit of the nature of mind. That total relaxation and abandonment is what is called 'neduwa' and the best metaphor to describe neduwa is, the moments of exhaustion after the ejaculation of sexual orgasm. That's the imperative neduwa state at the completion of every session of khorde rushen.

The Wheel of Desire

The wheel of life is one of the most common painted icons in Tibetan culture. It is frequently found in the portico of gompas. It depicts the basic elements of buddhist psychology, the modes of possible rebirth and the way out of samsara. The primary six-fold section of the wheel delineated according to six colors and six modes of rebirth can, in its detail, be interpreted in various ways. Here the six modes are given a psychological interpretation, dwelling on the sexual aspects of the six modes of being, turning the wheel into the wheel of desire. The aim is not to produce a practical psychology, not even a practical buddhist psychology upon which a path of moral evolution could be based. The aim is to provide inspiration more as poetry as an alternative means of access to memory that can inspire the acting out in the formal rushen practice.

The tsokhor (bhavachakra) is common to all Tibetan buddhist schools. It gained its present form and popularity during the Red-hat supremacy. This series of highly subjective vignettes, written and published on the internet forty years ago, has been edited for a very practical purpose.

Desire as the cause of suffering is at the root of all buddhist exegesis. The four noble truths which the buddha Sakyamuni expounded in his first sermon teach that all existence is suffering and that desire is the cause of suffering. He went on to show that suffering could be eliminated, or at least ameliorated, in human experience through the eightfold path of disciplined activity. Down the millennia buddhism developed various different methods of treating desire, but always desire was understood as the basic issue of human existence, and always desire was defined as the energy or life force that from the moment of conception to the moment of death reached out to hold and possess, to grasp and to cling to desirable objects. Within this definition, desire seeks to have and to hold all objects of sensory perception, but amongst them the one primary, universal drive of the life force is sexual – sexual desire is the principal root of suffering and the wheel of life describes the various forms that sexual desire takes.

The wheel of life spins fast and furious particularly in youth, when we can be sitting on top of the world one minute and find ourselves cast out in a lonely alienated space of anger and hatred in the next. And particularly in adolescence the emotional changes in the process are driven by sexual instinct and the emotional charge has a sexual source. The feeling of self-assurance in a beautiful world is most likely to arise out of a sense of sexual fulfilment in which a youthful, sensitive body-mind is flattered by love, endearments and sensual ministration. The greater the sense of self-admiration and self-congratulation the more intense is the pain of loss when our love object is sharing the pleasure with someone else. Jealousy obsesses the mind completely. Cut off from the love object and any chance of satisfaction, the mean head we are in gets negative reaction from alternative partners, and frustration is amplified. The anguish of this bind turns the whole world black and even friends appear as enemies and their ordinary remarks like wounding darts. Oblivious rage and violence against people or things comprise one possible exit from this trap, and we spin into a calculating self-serving world where we prey on our friends and enemies alike. When this catharsis is complete, energy subsided, we can return to humanity again to find the possibility of love and responsiveness. These are stages in the cycle of adolescent love-attachment and the wheel can go full circle in a minute, an hour or a day.

So the wheel of life can be articulated as the wheel of sexual desire and attachment. Life-force, lust for life and sex with a voracious appetite for pleasure, is its engine, and the whole gamut of emotion is its spin-off. As we grow older our sexual habit patterns become set, our sexual preferences more explicit, and it becomes evident which emotion, which mind-set on the wheel of sex-attachment, dominates. We can get stuck in a single state for days, months or even years, and accordingly our sexual personalities approximate one of the archetypes that define us socially and sexually. We are the perpetual virgin or the victim, the sensualist, the contender, the sexual junky, the demon, the predator – or the yogi of buddha-love. These labels denote psychosexual types, sexual personality types. Each personality type is dominated by a particular nasty emotion that seeping into sex life forms a tyrannical psychosexual complex. These emotions, specifically, are anxiety, pride, lust, jealousy, anger, and fear.

The Perpetual Virgin
The buddhist view places anxiety at the root of all our psyches, and the fear that it engenders is seen as the primary mind poison. Our sexual responses arise out of that fear. It is established in our sense of separation, our aloneness, that arises at birth with departure from the oneness with our mother in the womb into an alien world. As we grow up and our consciousness matures we are increasingly aware of our isolation and separation from the outside. 'I' is cut off from 'it', 'us' from 'the other', 'us' from 'the enemy', and looking at the world from inside a bubble, anxiety arises with all our perceptions. When something threatening is perceived outside, when 'it', 'the other', 'the unknown', threatens to invade our space, then anxiety spirals and adrenaline pumps into our body-mind. When the unknown is a horny man or woman threatening invasion of our bodies, the fear creates a wall of protection that seals us off from their advances.

The virgin, uncertain of his/her sexual identity, is only too well aware of this mechanism, but it afflicts – and protects

– all of us. Whenever we find ourselves in a state of uncertainty, unsure of our personal, social and sexual identity, anxiety seeps into the mind. If our sense of self is unformed, as in youth, then we need to climb the mountain of mind in order to gain a sense of who we are. We cannot engage sexually unless there is enough confidence to banish this basic anxiety. And ego-loss is only possible after the ego has been formed and possesses a strong sense of self and, in the same way, orgasm is unattainable until a threshold of tension is reached beyond which relaxation allows release and ejaculation. If our egos are formed, as in adulthood, but a sense of inferiority or low self-esteem undermines us, again we are a prey to the anxiety that inhibits sexual engagement.

Sexual abuse in childhood, painful or traumatic adolescent experience, repeated rejection, unhappy relationships, any of these can induce the anxiety that reinforces a habitual negative response to sexual advances. Desire is not strong enough to break through the resistance and rejection becomes an automatic response. Desire is repressed and an unwanted or at least an equivocal celibacy is enforced. External circumstances can arise, however, in which barriers are broken down – by alcohol, by perception of total security with a partner that causes an unusual boost in self-confidence – and the paralysis is relaxed. Loss of virginity can then occur, but in that experience impotence, premature ejaculation and orgasmic failure is possible. Take away the external conditions and we are back to the old syndrome of perpetual virginity and wallflower-mind. If our straight sexual drive is constantly frustrated by anxiety, if fear of the opposite sex is an insuperable obstacle to fulfilment, then the flow of desire can be sidelined towards the less threatening option of same sex attachment, and a gay habit is formed. Lack of experience can lead to arrest of our sexual development and we can get stuck in nonthreatening pre-adolescent practice resorting to sex with children. We also take refuge in the self-love and narcissism that makes masturbation the habitual mode of release.

Anxiety arises together with every sexual response, but the irrepressible, undeniable, emotion of lust, supported by pride and jealousy, dissolves or overwhelms it. If inhibiting factors prevent this process, the straight heterosexual drive is sidelined. But there is another way out – taking on the victim syndrome. Both male and female perpetual virgins can fall into this trap, but since nature endows woman with the weaker physique and provides her with more passive and submissive propensity, her greater vulnerability makes her more susceptible to it. The victim need do nothing more than obey, allowing her rejectionist tendencies to be overruled, taking no responsibility for her actions. If she has a history of abuse in childhood, rape or rough treatment to body or mind somewhere down the line – any sexual experience that destroys self-esteem – then the syndrome is already partly formed. She can fall victim to any of the psychosexual types: to the sensualist who will use her as a toy and as an erotic stimulant, to the contender who demands utter obedience and keeps total control of her, to the sexual junky who unleashes his frustration on her, to the sadistic demon who may take her to the bottom of her basest leanings, and to the predator who takes her and abandons her at will. The victim may make an unequal marriage wherein she is used and abused or she may be forced into the meanest option, which is prostitution.

The Sensualists or Gods of Love

Love is a sure means of dissolving anxiety and breaking through the paralytic effects of fear. It is an antidote to the mind poison of fear. To be loved is to feel sexually secure and induces the trust in which sexual mutuality can arise. We lose inhibition. To be in love is an outgoing state where physical giving and taking are a joy. In this state we can fulfil our own and our partners sexual needs and indulge our sensual whims. It may not be on the first night, in the nuptial bed, that things come together, but in the honeymoon phase of a marriage or a love affair the time and means exist for exploration and experimentation that leads to an understanding of, and then a reflexive physical response to, each other's needs and preferences. Erotic predilections are revealed, erogenous zones explored, sexual positions tested, and the most satisfying parameters of time and space delimited – all of this as an end in itself rather than as a means of establishing a fixed pattern of behavior. With increasing knowledge of each other's body-minds our sexual identities are focused, and this increases the self-assurance, boosts self-esteem, raises self-confidence and creates the ambience for developing the basics of erotic love that have already been established.

Perhaps, at this point, if we are confident enough in ourselves then the emotional element of the relationship becomes less significant. We are caught in the simple sensory intensity of touch and sensation through foreplay and physical union which are prolonged and extended to hours in daily multiple sessions of dalliance. Sex and love are the reason for being and become the priority in life. We cherish and flatter each other's beauty. Our bodies come alive in previously unimagined ways. We are made whole through the mutual giving and taking of our bodies and sexual fluids. Orgasm gives us a taste of divine pleasure, and mutual satisfaction an intimation of the divine totality of being. Fantasy is fulfilled – what we actually do is our fantasy immediately realized. Mutual adoration heightens the sense of being a god and a goddess in a sensual paradise. Because we cannot prevent an overflow of joy out of our bubble of union – and everyone loves a lover – our paradisiacal state of being is socially reinforced.

How long can this last? When does the rot set in? How long does it take to become jaded? How long before love is undermined by personality incompatibilities? How long before the rough and tumble of daily interaction creates niggling doubts and fears and seeds of distrust? It can be an hour or a lifetime, but eventually that initial glow of innocent pleasure declines. Most likely it is an inflated sense of self that heralds that loss. We become ego-bloated, thinking that it is 'I' who is creating the situation. Vanity intrudes. We become shameless in our love making, all sense of humility in the face of the great enigma of love lost, and we flaunt our sex to our partner and to the world in general. There is no longer freshness or purity in sensual exploration and the bloom of love fades. Driven by conditioned habit and the drive to repossess the highs of the honeymoon phase, we continue with the same uninhibited passion but our senses are jaded. To others our hubris is ugly and we lose social credibility and support.

Still with undeflatable pride and self-assurance, with a regular input of pleasure, we are hanging in that realm of divine pleasure, and we join the ranks of career sensualists. We no longer need our first little lover and variety in sexual experience becomes the spice of pleasure. And so we become stuck in a sensual paradise with a succession of lovers – or spouses – who provide more of the same satisfaction and also, to some degree, emotional fulfilment. We become sexual aristocrats, prima donnas, stars and starlets, practiced and easy in a sybaritic milieu, someone lucky in love. This is the world of the playboy and his mistress, the courtesan, and the geisha. We take all this for granted and become disdainful of a partner who still has a modicum of shame and consequent inhibition. The mass of sexual neurotics is treated with contempt and to the jaded sybarite the urge to play power-games with lesser gods and mere mortals susceptible to jealousy or driven to competition is a pleasure. No pity or compassion modifies such attitudes or ameliorates the rules of the games, and our partners suffer. We use and abuse the opposite sex as our playthings, as whores or gigolos. A shamelessness that may appear to others as lewd and lascivious distinguishes our sexual activity. We take multiple partners or design bacchanalian orgies for greater erotic stimulation. Any aperture is as good as another for penetration and gratification. Bisexuality is a recourse for the jaded appetite, and release through anal and oral sex are goals rather than aspects of foreplay. The charms of virgins, youth, and exotic partners may be particularly alluring and enticing. The dogmas of the Marquis de Sade can become our creed in order to arrest the inevitable decline into bodily decay and mental disillusion.

The Contenders

The honeymoon phase of love lasts only so long as the fabric of the relationship remains whole. When cracks appear in the mutuality of sexual engagement, when perceived inequalities emerge, gaps in reciprocal giving and taking, misunderstandings of motive and intent, love is faulted and consequent distrust gives space for real or imagined jealousies. Jealousy develops out of mistrust. There need be no third party involved here. If we doubt our partner's motivation then our jealousy shows at first simply as a constant vigilance accompanied by defensiveness. If the cracks in our love persist then this anxious attentiveness turns to possessiveness which may be driven by love but is counterproductive and increases the tension in the space between us and our partner. In this space competitiveness develops. If we are the object of jealousy, we perceive an emotional advantage over our possessive and defensive partner and exploit it. If we are the one tainted by jealousy, then our partner's dominance increases the distrust and our jealousy is exacerbated and we need a sense of control to counteract the underlying insecurity. The stage is now set for a war of the sexes for control and domination. Some form of degenerate love is still present, forming glue to the relationship, and that attachment – or perhaps it is the memory of a more generous phase of the relationship – excludes the possibility of just walking away.

Still recalling the sense of power and divine satiation of the honeymoon phase, still self-satisfied and smug in our memory of those godlike moments, we are now bitter at the loss of it. Feeling threatened in the space of separation we resort to our ego as refuge, elevating ourselves and putting down our partner and adversary with contempt and disdain. Verbal and physical confrontation punctuate the relationship. We spin webs of intrigue enlisting allies in the war. The woman in the relationship, with sensitive susceptibility to jealousy – and hell hath no fury like a woman scorned – eating her heart out in this era of feminism can enlist an army of womanhood on her side and the engagement becomes a gender war in which the threat of the lesbian option may become an invidious strategic weapon. Other love objects or sexual partners may be brought into the engagement as tactical weapons. The male, though, pushed out of his equanimity, increasingly takes refuge in an atavistic macho mind set to combat the woman's wiles, which in its turn drives her to greater excesses.

All this jealous contention may prohibit sexual engagement. But it was only yesterday that we were satisfying each other nightly with intuitive and sensitive mutual response, and from habit and desire energized by combat the battle may take on physical and emotional forms in bed. Here the passion of jealousy is transposed onto desire, and mutual embitterment becomes reciprocal stimulation and satisfaction. The urge to control focuses attention on techniques of seduction, arousal and release, which refine and sophisticate foreplay and union. Such techniques may be refined in sadomasochistic games in which both partners are gratified in turn through domination and submission. But such moments of rapprochement and mutual gratification become less frequent as the spiral of combat widens and the greater distance between the partners induces the distrust that is indistinguishable from paranoia, and it is time for separation or divorce.

The habit of contention will follow us out of the formative relationship and into the arena of search for another partner. Here the drive behind our ambition to succeed and win, not only in sexual competition but in all aspects of life, will be seen as a desirable quality by a similarly ambitious partner. But if our luck runs out and we are rejected by our chosen lover, jilted for a friend perhaps, and then our next best choice abandons us for a peer in the rat race, the old propensity for jealousy is inflamed in a loveless, lonely space, where we can easily become caught and stuck with a jealous obsession. Envy of those still swanning around in their sybaritic milieu of mutual gratification is like a barb in our flesh. Here we are the embittered cynic who reflexively bursts other people's balloons, frustrates their designs, sinks their deals, imputes the negative motivation, and tries to outmaneuver them at every turn in a constant game of one-upmanship. Sex with its politics is a loveless game here, played with a merciless disregard for the feelings of the competition. Honing political and verbal skills in this dance of jealousy and envy we become the politico on the sexual scene, the sexual manipulator, the player obsessed by defeating the competition and taking the prize. But during the proceedings a creeping paranoia compels us to glance constantly over our shoulders to guard our back and we trip ourselves up with suspicion. We are increasingly alienated, and with this sense of exclusion from society and the opposite sex our frustration and craving escalate.

Sexual Junkies

The sexual junky is addicted to sex as if it were the elixir of life. He is obsessed by his desire to the exclusion of all else. But he cannot connect. He *must* have it, but he cannot get it. The intensity of his insatiable craving frustrates gratification. If through divine intervention he does get it, he cannot find satisfaction. He wanders invisibly in constant search of relief in a sexual desert empty of romance, eroticism and sensual pleasure. The gross intensity of his need makes him repugnant to many potential partners. If he does find a woman who pities him, or who lacks discrimination, and will give it to him, his imperative lust, his one-track self-directed obsession, turns her off. If she can ignore his pathetic urgency, foreplay is a ghastly self-conscious ritual and his frantic desire leaves him impotent. If his automatic sexual mechanism allows him an erection he is denied penetration. If eventually he succeeds, his orgasm is premature or despite desperate prolonged and arduous effort he cannot attain it. If he does ejaculate there is no satisfaction in the act, no gratification and no remission of desire. His partner is distressed and unsatisfied and he is left to wander the sexual desert alone again in chagrin. Although virtually invisible to others he can see their romance, their erotic interplay, and their mutual gratification, which further inflames his unsated lust. His recourse to masturbation is thwarted by the same mechanisms, and also by the ineffectiveness of his sexual fantasies, and it leaves him only with greater desire.

The female junky is similarly afflicted, wandering the badlands in search of gratification. Her craving inhibits display of the subtle signs and body language that would attract appropriate partners. Her one-track obsession makes her ugly and offensive. But since her role in the sexual dance is more passive and men are less interested in her state of mind than her genitals, she still succeeds in attracting potential partners. Her inappropriate verbal responses, hard edged, self-piteous or lascivious, turn off a majority of those she attracts but still she has the opportunity for sex. But she is utterly insatiable and no quantity or intensity of action will gratify her. Satisfying orgasm and catharsis is for her impossible, although any slight intimation of potential pleasure will drive her to frantic effort toward fulfilment. The urgency of her physical need is accompanied by peremptory demands. Inflamed and unsatisfied by one sexual act, with or without a partner, she immediately seeks another. Sex is the only activity that gives meaning to her sense of existence. She is a nympho.

The cause of this frustrated sexual craving seems not to arise out of fear – though fear may be at its root – so much as alienation. We feel ourselves to be cut off, enisled, isolated beyond bearing. When our sexual drive has been stimulated and intensified by emotional and sexual engagement and we are deprived of the source of our gratification through rejection in love or sexual failure, or just by a hiatus in a relationship, we are left with a heightened sense of self and a looming consciousness of the gap that separates us from our erstwhile partner. Infidelity is one efficient way of driving space between ourselves and a committed partner. By seeking to reestablish the relationship, by grasping and clinging, we only push the love-object further away and a vicious cycle of craving is endured – the more we crave and yearn, the greater the distance between us and the greater the need for union. The sexual junky mistakes emotional and spiritual fulfilment for sexual release, and since some significant human communication must preface sexual engagement, union is unattainable.

But before obsessional lust dominates us completely, and before fulfillment is reflexively thwarted by a one-track pursuit of sexual release and orgasm, we can resort to extremes of sexual stimulation to arouse us. The connection between violence and sex can be exploited in sadomaso-chism, and at the extreme of impotence and frustration inflicting or suffering physical pain is a means to arousal. Acting out sexual fantasies, like bondage or infantile regression, can be used by the sexual junky to excite the jaded senses or inhibited sexuality in order to eke out some small sexual release and gratification. Our partner may be a sexual junky of the opposite sex who is susceptible to our needs and who indeed may welcome attention, but it may also be a vulnerable victim upon whom we may unleash the full force of frustrated lust.

Devils (Hell-beings)

Frustrated craving is released by relaxation into a level of common human awareness where communication with other beings is restored and mutuality in sexual relationship is again possible. But what if that relaxation escapes us and the vicious cycle of desire and separation continues to focus consciousness on our self as an isolated, cut off entity? Since no one and no thing out there give us any sense of freedom and we are unable to discern even a germ of sympathy, an aversion to the entire world arises and to everyone in it. Anger at the injustice of our misery compared to others' happiness turns us bitter and acrimonious. Alone and alienated from the world and humanity we are afraid, and a grain of fear enters into every moment of perception poisoning us to any positive input. We begin to hate, not only what is hateful but whatever arises in the senses. Paranoia sets in.

If we are still in a relationship when fear and anger possess us then our partner is going to bear the brunt of our pain. We mistake the ministrations of our sympathetic partner for the goading of an enemy and we react viciously. We want to punish our lover for precipitating this state. The 'other' is to blame. We express our alienation, our anger and fear, in verbal abuse, or mental persecution, sexually excommunicating him/her, refusing and denying communication. Projecting our own mind set upon our partner we react as if he/she had consciously given us AIDS, perceiving him/her as a demon out there, torturing us, seeking to inflict the maximum amount of pain on us. This is the reflexive reaction of the paranoid unable to distinguish between the delusory hell of his/her own making and the reality outside. If we possess an inkling of the miserable inappropriateness of our actions, we rage at the bind we are in, setting off another round of vicious behavior.

In this state of acute aversion and fear there is no possibility of mutual sexual engagement. It is a state of sexual paralysis. But this numbness of sexual response can easily be broken. When fear and hatred spiral beyond the tolerance of consciousness our anger becomes physical violence – here are the wife-beater and the flailing, berserk lover – and violence is a sexual stimulant and rape the form it takes. At the end of his tether, the demon is the sadist, the rapist, the sexual killer and the snuff-video creator.

The Predators
The hell of paranoid fear and anger also passes. The wheel turns, and emerging out of that black hole, we rebound from excessive aversion into the shadowy world of the predator. Our rage has burnt itself out, and impulsive, destructive urges are sated. In their place is an instinctual drive to survive and a brute cunning. Our sexual drive is uninhibited and uncontrolled. We are devoid of self-esteem and we lack any moral sensibility or discrimination, so woman or man, anal or oral sex, are equally acceptable in this bisexual sphere. The male can use his brute strength to take what he needs. An implied threat of physical violence is enough to effect initial physical intimidation. This type of sex is brute lust. In this twilight world the perpetual virgin is particularly vulnerable.

The predatory male takes whatever partner he can dominate. His bonded partner is the most accessible victim. If he is without a partner then a woman with a similar absence of self-esteem in a similar state of arousal is accessible, as in this instinctual state we have pheromonal hypersensitive to and are naturally attracted to partners of like mind – the predator is not necessarily a rapist. Sex workers, male or female, cater to the predator who has some relational sensitivity. Whoever the female partner, she will be used without compunction or constraint on an instinctual level of gross sex, with orgasm and ejaculation the one-pointed goal. The male caught in this state learns to use his physical strength to his advantage, identifies the victim like a lion his prey, rejects any foreplay taking his partner with him, and concludes the sexual act in a very short time, probably with premature ejaculation.

The female predator in this state is the unfettered pornographic woman, displaying her sex grossly and focused only on the satisfaction of being inseminated. But she can be as cunning as the male in her hunting, the virago feeding off the innocent and/or stupid male. Physical strength is not her weapon, although size and energy intensity may equally serve to intimidate a male victim. But more likely it is with her keen calculating mind that she seduces him, the spider luring the fly into the web. Once her desire is sated he is abandoned, thrown onto the heap of her rejects. Like a vampire she sucks him dry of the sexual fluids that give her vitality and then discards him, and like a vampire's victim he is conditioned to follow her method in the future.

The Human Realm: The Rare Opportunity

In the same way that some animals can be domesticated and their 'survival of the fittest', 'kill or be killed' instinct overridden by the promise of safety and security, so the sexual predator can be socialized by the promise of greater pleasure to be attained through relational sensitivity and consequent mutuality. We may go through a similar process when we have been lost in a fog of inertia and sloth, where our sexual responses are lazy and blunted, our pleasure curtailed, and where relationships are difficult to create. Through the intervention of a new potential partner a window is opened upon the pleasure of a refined, eroticized sexuality with a moral sensibility and a satisfying emotional aspect, and this carrot dangled in front of us is enough to vitalize our sexuality propelling us into another dimension of satisfaction.

In this thoroughly human dimension there is emotional security and we can relax and explore the possibilities of sexual relationship. Here we can train ourselves physically, with yoga or calisthenics, and experiment with different sexual postures, modes, breathing, decreasing or increasing the period of sexual engagement, and so on. Inside and outside the bedroom we are more aware of the nuances of gender relationship and the benefits that sensitive and selfless response can give, and our consciousness of this dimension of sexuality is broadened and heightened. In this process of sensitization and socialization some guilt and shame at our past selfishness and viciousness can be useful in motivating us toward a state where mutuality flourishes. Some lovers may become stuck in this process of sexual training, where sexual engagement is a nice physical ritual without any chance of spontaneity. But if this pitfall is avoided, sexuality developed and matured through self-development, we arrive in a space where a potential partner beckons from a paradise of sensuality, heightened pleasure and joyful satisfaction. Most of us will take this option and move into another cycle on the wheel of desire. Others will say 'Enough!', 'Never again!' and take the path of the tantric buddha.

Recommended Texts

Chokgyur Lingpa and Jamyang Khyentse Wangpo. *The Light of Wisdom Vol IV*: trans: Erik Pema Kunzang. Rangjung Yeshe Pub. 2001. Restricted.

Keith Dowman, *Yeshe Lama*, Dzogchen Now! Books, 2014 Amazon.com.

Nyoshul Khen Rinpoche, "Principles of the Dzogchen Practice of Khordé Rushen." www.lotsawahouse.org A highly regarded disciple of Dudjom Rinpoche provides an excellent summary of the principles of khorde rushen, in the graduated context.

Radical Dzogchen Teaching Series
Dzogchen Now! Books : Available on Amazon

Semdzins

Nonmeditation

SAMAYA

Mahamudra

Khorde Rushen

Forthcoming

The Dzogchen View

Daily Ritual

Pilgrimage

Made in the USA
Monee, IL
08 October 2020

44417534R00049